The Ultimate  Sandwich

35 Breakfast Sandwiches You Can Make At Home With A Breakfast Sandwich Maker

By: Jennifer Williams

ISBN-13 978-1491077030

TABLE OF CONTENTS

4 NOT JUST FOR BREAKFAST   45

Jennifer Williams

Paperback Edition

Manufactured in the United States of America

ACKNOWLEDGMENT

For my Mother who always made sure I started my day off right with a great breakfast.

INTRODUCTION

Just forget about skipping breakfast. Breakfast is the most important meal of the day. Yet, it often is the hardest meal to fit into your schedule or to know what to prepare.

College students, busy moms, teenagers and so many people on the go find it either too time consuming or cumbersome to make breakfast for themselves.

With these delicious recipes and a small pan or cooking appliance, your morning meal couldn't be quicker or more delicious. With a breakfast sandwich maker, these recipes are even easier to make, ready in 5 minutes and clean-up is a breeze.

If you are one of those people who know that a good breakfast is the way to start your day but struggle for time and ideas on what to make, we know you will enjoy this fun and fast way to make a delicious breakfast sandwich.

The Ultimate Breakfast Sandwich

A great breakfast gives your body essential fuel and nutrients to power you through the day. Breakfast gives you an energy boost, powers the brain and helps you to lose weight or keep it off. Many of the traditional breakfast ingredients include protein, vitamins A and D and antioxidants which are essential to your overall health.

Top this off with your favorite juice, a glass of milk, and an amazing cup of coffee and you should be ready to kick off your day.

You will never have to skip breakfast again...

CHAPTER 1- BREAKFAST SANDWICH 101

Breakfast Sandwich Maker: The recipes in this book have been designed to work with a breakfast sandwich maker. You will find some of the directions very similar between recipes. That is because it really just takes a few simple steps to get your sandwich ready to eat. Also, I personally do not like reading a recipe that continually refers me back to the appliance manufacturer's instructions of some other random place – I want it all in one spot – hopefully you will too.

Other Cooking Methods: These recipes can also be prepared with other small kitchen appliances such as an all-in-one griddle or sandwich maker or your good old fashioned pots and pans. You will just need to alter the directions accordingly and it will take longer to prepare.

Utensils and tools: We recommend using nylon or any other non-metal utensil when using your sandwich maker or with any pan to avoid scratching and damaging the surface. You can also use wood utensils, but they are not my favorite because of the potential for retaining flavors and bacteria.

Ingredients: In our recipes we occasionally use a specific brand of ingredient in the recipe. We have done this for a few reasons; the consistency and flavor of the product works well with the recipe; the product is all-natural, contains less artificial and processed ingredients, or is gluten free; the ingredient fits well with the ideal breakfast sandwich.

You can always, of course, substitute with your favorite ingredients, local brand or whatever you have on hand in the kitchen.

CHAPTER 2- CLASSIC BREAKFAST SANDWICHES

The Classic

"Just like the famous fast food version but from the comfort of your home and made with your own choice of quality ingredients.

Servings: 1

Prep Time: 3 Minutes

Cook Time: 5 Minutes

Per Serving: 306 Calories | 27.6g Carbohydrates | 12.6g Fat | 20.3g Protein

INGREDIENTS:

1 English muffin, cut in half

1 slice Canadian bacon

1 slice American cheese

1 egg

DIRECTIONS:

Preheat breakfast sandwich maker.

Place one-half muffin, split side up, into bottom ring of breakfast sandwich maker. Add 1 slice each of Canadian bacon and American cheese.

Lower cooking plate and top ring. Add egg. Pierce top of egg with a toothpick or pointed plastic utensil. Top with remaining muffin half, split side down.

Close cover. Cook 4 – 5 minutes. Gently rotate cooking plate handle away clockwise. Lift rings. Remove breakfast sandwich with a plastic or nylon spatula.

Bacon, Avocado and Cheddar

"Avocadoes add such creamy goodness to any recipe. Choose avocados with firm skin and no soft spots. They should be firm but with a gently give when pressed.

Servings: 1

Prep Time: 5 Minutes

Cook Time: 5 Minutes

Per Serving: 594 Calories | 36.5g Carbohydrates |38.6g Fat | 27.4g Protein

INGREDIENTS:

2 slices multi-grain bread, cut into rounds

2 slices thick cut bacon, cooked

1 slice sharp cheddar

1/4 Avocado, sliced

1 slice red onion

1 Tbsp Aioli

1 large egg

DIRECTIONS:

Preheat breakfast sandwich maker.

Place slice of whole grain bread, into bottom ring of breakfast sandwich maker. Add bacon, sharp cheddar cheese, avocado slices and red onion.

Lower cooking plate and top ring. Add egg. Pierce top of egg with a toothpick or pointed plastic utensil.

Spread remaining slice of bread with Aioli (or other favorite topping). Place spread side down on top of egg.

Close cover. Cook 4 – 5 minutes. Gently rotate cooking plate handle away clockwise. Lift rings. Remove breakfast sandwich with a plastic or nylon spatula.

Breakfast Melt

"Inspired by the Classic but with an updated twist on ingredients for a delightful morning treat: cherrywood smoked bacon, Fontina cheese and fresh sage.

Servings: 1

Prep Time: 5 Minutes

Cook Time: 5 Minutes

Per Serving: 520 Calories | 29.1g Carbohydrates |31.1g Fat | 31.6g Protein

INGREDIENTS:

2 ounces Fontina cheese, sliced

2 slices Nueske's Cherrywood bacon, cooked

1 English muffin, split

1 large farm-fresh egg

1 sprig fresh sage

DIRECTIONS:

Preheat breakfast sandwich maker.

Cook bacon in oven for maximum crispness and minimal greasiness, or use your preferred method. Cut bacon slices in half.

Place one slice English muffin in bottom ring of breakfast sandwich maker. Top with Fontina and bacon.

Lower cooking plate and top ring. Add egg. Pierce top of egg with a toothpick or pointed plastic utensil. Top with sage. Place muffin on top.

Close cover. Cook 4 – 5 minutes. Gently rotate cooking plate handle away clockwise. Lift rings. Remove breakfast sandwich with a plastic, nylon or wooden spatula.

Rustic Ham and Cheese Sandwich

"This country home-style sandwich is made with some of Wisconsin's finest.

Servings: 1

Prep Time: 5 Minutes

Cook Time: 5 Minutes

Per Serving: 331 Calories | 26.5g Carbohydrates |14.6g Fat | 21.9g Protein

INGREDIENTS:

2 slices (1/2-inch thick) Rustic white country bread

1 slices (1 ounce) Wisconsin Gruyere or Swiss cheese

2 Jones Ham Slices

1 slice, (1 ounce) Wisconsin Brick cheese

1 egg

1 tablespoon fresh Rosemary, chopped (optional)

DIRECTIONS:

Preheat breakfast sandwich maker.

Place one slice rustic white bread in bottom ring of breakfast sandwich maker. Top with 1 slice Gruyere cheese and 2 slices ham. Sprinkle lightly with fresh chopped rosemary. Top with 1 slice Brick cheese.

Lower cooking plate and top ring. Add egg to top of ring and pierce yolk. Sprinkle fresh rosemary on top of egg. Top with remaining slice of rustic white bread.

The Ultimate Breakfast Sandwich

Close cover. Cook 4 – 5 minutes. Gently rotate cooking plate handle away clockwise. Lift rings. Remove breakfast sandwich with a plastic or nylon spatula.

Sausage Crust Spinach Parmesan Quiche

"Quiche? Yes, easy scrumptious single-serving quiche from your sandwich maker. . .

Servings: 1

Prep Time: 10 Minutes

Cook Time: 5 Minutes

Per Serving: 462 Calories | 5.8g Carbohydrates |36.3g Fat | 30.0g Protein

INGREDIENTS:

1 Jones All Natural Mild Pork Sausage Patty (fully cooked)

1 Tbsp butter

2 Tbsp yellow onion, chopped

1 ounce frozen chopped spinach, thawed

Pinch ground nutmeg

1 ounce Mozzarella cheese, grated

1 Tbsp Parmesan cheese, grated

1 egg

1 Tbsp half and half

Salt & pepper to taste

DIRECTIONS:

Preheat breakfast sandwich maker.

Place sausage patty into bottom ring of breakfast sandwich maker.

The Ultimate Breakfast Sandwich

Melt butter in medium sauté pan and add chopped onions. Cook for about 3 minutes or until soft and translucent.

Meanwhile, squeeze excess moisture from thawed spinach until dry and crumbly. Stir spinach into onions and cook mixture for another 2 - 3 minutes. Add nutmeg and season with salt and pepper to taste. Remove from heat and add Parmesan cheese.

Spread spinach mixture over sausage crust. Place sausage spinach patty into bottom ring of breakfast sandwich maker. Sprinkle shredded mozzarella on top.

In small bowl, beat 1 egg together with half and half.

Lower cooking plate and top ring. Add beaten egg to top ring.

Close cover. Cook 4 – 5 minutes. Gently rotate cooking plate handle away clockwise. Lift rings. Remove breakfast quiche with a plastic or nylon spatula.

Chorizo and Cheese Breakfast Sandwich

"Spanish influenced breakfast to give your day a kick-start.

Servings: 1

Prep Time: 5 Minutes

Cook Time: 5 Minutes

Per Serving: 496 Calories | 30.7g Carbohydrates |30.7g Fat | 23.5g Protein

INGREDIENTS:

1 round Baguette, sliced in half

1 Johnsonville Chorizo Sausage patty, cooked

1 slice American or Cheddar cheese

1 medium egg

DIRECTIONS:

Preheat breakfast sandwich maker.

Place one-half baguette, split side up, into bottom ring of breakfast sandwich maker. Add Chorizo sausage patty and cheese.

Lower cooking plate and top ring. Add egg. Pierce top of egg with a toothpick or pointed plastic utensil.

Top with remaining baguette half, split side down.

Close cover. Cook 4 – 5 minutes. Gently rotate cooking plate handle away clockwise. Lift rings. Remove breakfast sandwich with a plastic or nylon spatula.

Waffles and Sausage Sandwich

"Another great take on a breakfast tradition made into a sandwich.

Servings: 1

Prep Time: 5 Minutes

Cook Time: 5 Minutes

Per Serving: 443 Calories | 32.4g Carbohydrates |28.4g Fat | 17.6g Protein

INGREDIENTS:

2 waffles, round from frozen

1 maple pork sausage patty

1 egg

Maple syrup (optional)

DIRECTIONS:

Preheat breakfast sandwich maker.

Optional: toast waffles for a slightly crisper sandwich.

Place one waffle into bottom ring of breakfast sandwich maker. Add sausage patty.

Lower cooking plate and top ring. Add egg. Pierce top of egg with a toothpick or pointed plastic utensil.

Top with remaining waffle.

Close cover. Cook 4 – 5 minutes. Gently rotate cooking plate handle away clockwise. Lift rings. Remove breakfast sandwich with a plastic or nylon spatula. Serve with maple syrup.

Zesty Bologna Breakfast Sandwich

"Any brand of onion relish will work well for this sandwich. Just choose the flavors you like or make your own.

Servings: 1

Prep Time: 1 Minute

Cook Time: 5 Minutes

Per Serving: 195 Calories | 22.5g Carbohydrates |8.5g Fat | 6.7g Protein

INGREDIENTS:

2 slices rye bread

1 slice Bologna

Dijon mustard

2 Tbsp onion relish

1 egg

DIRECTIONS:

Preheat breakfast sandwich maker.

Spread lower rye bread with Dijon mustard. Place one slice, mustard side up, into bottom ring of breakfast sandwich maker. Add slice Bologna. Top with onion relish.

Lower cooking plate and top ring. Add egg and pierce yolk. Top with remaining slice of rye bread, mustard side down.

Close cover. Cook 4 – 5 minutes. Gently rotate cooking plate handle away clockwise. Lift rings. Remove breakfast sandwich with a plastic or nylon spatula.

Apple Bacon and Cheddar Croissant

"Use tart apples such as a Granny Smith or Fiji to complement the bacon and sharp cheddar flavors. You can also microwave the apple slices with the brown sugar and butter to add caramel apple goodness to your croissant.

Servings: 1

Prep Time: 5 Minutes

Cook Time: 5 Minutes

Per Serving: 572 Calories | 24.4g Carbohydrates |39.2g Fat | 29.8g Protein

INGREDIENTS:

1 small croissant, cut in half

1 pork sausage patty

1/4 tart green apple, thinly sliced

2 tbsp sharp cheddar, shredded

1 tsp brown sugar

1 egg

DIRECTIONS:

Preheat breakfast sandwich maker.

Place bottom of croissant, split side up, into bottom ring of breakfast sandwich maker. Add sausage patty. Layer apple slices on patty; sprinkle with brown sugar. Add sharp cheddar.

Lower cooking plate and top ring. Add egg. Pierce top of egg with a toothpick or pointed plastic utensil.

Top with top of croissant, split side down.

Close cover. Cook 4 – 5 minutes. Gently rotate cooking plate handle away clockwise. Lift rings. Remove breakfast sandwich with a nylon spatula.

Optional: Add apples, brown sugar and a tsp of butter to a small bowl; cover and microwave on high for 5 minutes to caramelize the apples; stir. Add to top of sausage patty in sandwich maker.

Hash Browns and Sausage

"Hearty hash brown, sausage and egg combination surely won't leave you feeling hungry. An often recommended antidote for a hangover.

Servings: 1

Prep Time: 10 Minutes

Cook Time: 5 Minutes

Per Serving: 631 Calories | 37g Carbohydrates |48.3g Fat | 19.1g Protein

INGREDIENTS:

2 Hash brown patties

1 sausage patty, cooked

1 slice American cheese

1 large egg

DIRECTIONS:

Preheat breakfast sandwich maker.

Cook hash brown patties according to package directions.

Place one hash brown patty bottom ring of breakfast sandwich maker. Add sausage patty and American cheese.

Lower cooking plate and top ring. Add egg. Pierce top of egg with a toothpick or pointed plastic utensil.

Top egg with remaining hash brown patty.

Close cover. Cook 4 – 5 minutes. Gently rotate cooking plate handle away clockwise. Lift rings. Remove breakfast sandwich with a plastic or nylon spatula.

CHAPTER 3 – VEGETARIAN

Meatless Egg and Cheese on Golden Biscuits

"Warm, flakey, buttery goodness without the meat. A breakfast sandwich doesn't get much easier than this.

Servings: 1

Prep Time: 1 Minute

Cook Time: 5 Minutes

Per Serving: 279 Calories | 18.4g Carbohydrates |16.8g Fat | 15.5g Protein

NGREDIENTS:

1 biscuit, sliced

1 slice mild cheddar

1 large egg

DIRECTIONS:

Preheat breakfast sandwich maker.

Place one-half biscuit, split side up, into bottom ring of breakfast sandwich maker. Add the mild cheddar cheese slice.

Lower cooking plate and top ring. Add egg. Pierce top of egg with a toothpick or pointed plastic utensil.

Top with remaining biscuit half, split side down.

Close cover. Cook 4 – 5 minutes. Gently rotate cooking plate handle away clockwise. Lift rings. Remove breakfast sandwich with a plastic or nylon spatula.

Chocolate Chip Blueberry Pancakes

"The good-anytime sandwich. The brie adds the right amount of creaminess to pull this all together.

Servings: 1

Prep Time: 5 Minutes

Cook Time: 5 Minutes

Per Serving: 303 Calories | 29.1g Carbohydrates |15.6g Fat | 13.2g Protein

INGREDIENTS:

2 pancakes, from frozen

1 tbsp blueberry preserves

1 tbsp mini dark chocolate chips

1 ounce Brie cheese, cut to 1 inch pieces

1 egg

Maple syrup (optional)

DIRECTIONS:

Preheat breakfast sandwich maker.

Place one-pancake into bottom ring of breakfast sandwich maker. Add Drop in blueberry preserves, chocolate chips and brie.

In a small bowl, lightly beat egg with fork. Lower cooking plate and top ring. Add beaten egg

Top with remaining pancake.

Close cover. Cook 4 – 5 minutes. Gently rotate cooking plate handle away clockwise. Lift rings. Remove breakfast sandwich with a plastic or nylon spatula.

Drizzle with your favorite syrup.

Fat Burning Breakfast Sandwich

"Kick off your morning with a satisfying treat that will burn the belly fat.

Servings: 1

Prep Time: 5 Minutes

Cook Time: 5 Minutes

Per Serving: 412 Calories | 21.7g Carbohydrates |29.9g Fat | 17.7g Protein

INGREDIENTS:

½ toasted whole grain English muffin

2 tsp. olive oil

¼ ripe Avocado

1 slice Swiss cheese

1 slice tomato

1 egg,

DIRECTIONS:

Preheat breakfast sandwich maker.

Drizzle olive oil over the English muffin. Place muffin into bottom ring of breakfast sandwich maker. Add the avocado, Swiss cheese and tomato.

Lower cooking plate and top ring. Add egg. Pierce top of egg with a toothpick or pointed plastic utensil. Sprinkle with pepper, if desired.

Close cover. Cook 4 – 5 minutes. Gently rotate cooking plate handle away clockwise. Lift rings. Remove breakfast sandwich with a plastic or nylon spatula.

Portabella Mushroom Sandwich

"Enjoy this meatless breakfast sandwich goodness with hearty portabella mushrooms and a creamy goat cheese. You can also eliminate the English muffin entirely and just use the mushroom as your 'muffin'. . .

Servings: 1

Prep Time: 12 Minutes

Cook Time: 5 Minutes

Per Serving: 437 Calories | 40.1g Carbohydrates |24.3g Fat | 18.7g Protein

INGREDIENTS:

1 whole grain English muffin

1 Portabella mushroom cap

1 ounce Chevre cheese

Extra virgin olive oil

Ground sage, pinch

Sea salt to taste

Pepper to taste

1/2 cup arugula

1 large egg

DIRECTIONS:

Preheat breakfast sandwich maker.

Spread one half of the goat cheese on one half of the muffin. Place muffin, cheese side up, into bottom ring of breakfast sandwich maker.

The Ultimate Breakfast Sandwich

Clean the Portabella mushroom, removing stem and gills. Brush the rounded side of the mushroom cap with olive oil. Sprinkle the gill side with the sage, pepper, and salt. Heat a small skillet over medium-high heat. Cook the mushroom cap, gill side up, covered for 3 minutes. Reduce heat to medium. Flip mushroom cap and cook, covered about 5 more minutes.

Place the mushroom, gill side up, on the muffin half in breakfast maker.

Lower cooking plate and top ring. Add egg. Pierce top of egg with a toothpick or pointed plastic utensil.

Close cover. Cook 4 – 5 minutes. Gently rotate cooking plate handle away clockwise. Lift rings. Remove breakfast sandwich with a plastic or nylon spatula.

Top with Arugula and remaining muffin half.

Caramelized Onion and Kale Frittata

"Kale is low fat, saturated fat free, cholesterol free, low sodium, an excellent source of vitamins A, C, K and B6 and a good source of calcium, potassium, copper and manganese. It is also a good source of dietary fiber, protein, thiamin, riboflavin, folate, iron, magnesium and phosphorus. Need we say more?

Servings: 1

Prep Time: 15 Minutes

Cook Time: 5 Minutes

Per Serving: 263 Calories | 5.7g Carbohydrates |19.0g Fat | 18.0g Protein

INGREDIENTS:

1 medium egg

1 medium egg white

2 tbsps Asiago cheese, shredded

1 cup Kale, washed well

1/2 cup white onion, sliced thin

2 tbsp butter

Salt and fresh pepper to taste

DIRECTIONS:

Preheat breakfast sandwich maker.

In a small bowl, blend egg, egg white and Asiago cheese.

Melt 1 tbsp butter in small skillet over low heat. Add onions and sauté until translucent. Raise heat to medium and continue sautéing onions until caramelized. Add to egg and cheese mixture.

Cut kale into small strips. Melt remaining tbsp butter in skillet. Add kale and cook until wilted, about 3 minutes. Add kale to egg mixture. Blend well.

Lower cooking plate and top ring.

Add egg mixture to top cooking plate.

Close cover. Cook 5 – 6 minutes, or until firm. Gently rotate cooking plate handle away clockwise. Lift rings. Remove frittata with a plastic or nylon spatula.

Florentine Eggs

"Simple, elegant, low calorie spinach and eggs with a light mustard-yogurt spread.

Servings: 1

Prep Time: 5 Minutes

Cook Time: 5 Minutes

Per Serving: 152 Calories | 15.4g Carbohydrates |5.3g Fat | 10.1g Protein

INGREDIENTS:

1/8 cup plain yogurt

1/4 teaspoon Dijon mustard

1 egg

1/2 English muffin

1/4 cup fresh baby spinach leaves

Salt and pepper to taste

DIRECTIONS:

Preheat breakfast sandwich maker.

Mix yogurt and mustard together. Spread on English muffin half.

Place muffin, yogurt side up, into bottom ring of breakfast sandwich maker. Add baby spinach leaves.

Lower cooking plate and top ring. Add egg. Pierce top of egg with a toothpick or pointed plastic utensil.

Close cover. Cook 4 – 5 minutes. Gently rotate cooking plate handle away clockwise. Lift rings. Remove breakfast sandwich with a plastic or nylon spatula.

Season to taste with salt and pepper.

Mediterranean Eggwhites Sandwich

"Spinach, roasted tomatoes and basil pesto bring a Mediterranean flair to your kitchen.

Servings: 1

Prep Time: 10 Minutes

Cook Time: 5 Minutes

Per Serving: 337 Calories | 30.7g Carbohydrates |17.5g Fat | 11.6g Protein

INGREDIENTS:

1 Ciabatta role, cut in half

1 slice white cheddar

1/4 cup spinach, chopped

1 small roasted tomato, drained and sliced

1 tbsp basil pesto

2 egg whites

DIRECTIONS:

Preheat breakfast sandwich maker.

Spread basil pesto on each half of Ciabatta role. Place one half role, pesto side up, into bottom ring of breakfast sandwich maker. Add spinach and roasted tomato. Lay white cheddar on top.

Whisk egg whites with fork. Lower cooking plate and top ring. Add egg whites to cooking plate.

Top with remaining Ciabatta role, pesto side down.

Close cover. Cook 4 – 5 minutes. Gently rotate cooking plate handle away clockwise. Lift rings. Remove breakfast sandwich with a plastic or nylon spatula.

Margherita Pizza

"Pizza for breakfast or just anytime at all. The classic Margherita Pizza can be enjoyed anytime and oh so easy...

Servings: 1

Prep Time: 10 Minutes

Cook Time: 5 Minutes

Per Serving: 492 Calories | 26.3g Carbohydrates |29.2g Fat | 37.5g Protein

INGREDIENTS:

1 flatbread round

2 oz Mozzarella, shredded

1 small tomato, diced

1 tbsp onion, chopped

1 tbsp fresh basil, chopped

1/8 tsp garlic powder

Pinch of dry oregano

1 tsp extra-virgin olive oil

1 egg

Parmesan cheese, grated (optional)

DIRECTIONS:

Preheat breakfast sandwich maker.

Brush flatbread lightly with olive oil. Place flatbread into bottom ring of breakfast sandwich maker. Add 2/3 of tomatoes to top of flatbread.

In a small skillet, heat olive oil. Sauté onion until translucent. Stir in basil, garlic powder and oregano. Remove from heat.

In a small bowl, whisk egg. Add sautéed onion mixture to egg.

Lower cooking plate and top ring. Add egg mixture to cooking plate.

Close cover. Cook 4 – 5 minutes. Gently rotate cooking plate handle away clockwise. Lift rings. Remove breakfast sandwich with a nylon spatula.

Top with remaining tomatoes. Sprinkle with parmesan cheese.

CHAPTER 4- NOT JUST FOR BREAKFAST

PROSCIUTTO, ARTICHOKES AND CREAM CHEESE ON A BRIOCHE

"The combinations of salty and sweet in this sandwich are rich and inviting.

Servings: 1

Prep Time: 5 Minutes

Cook Time: 5 Minutes

Per Serving: 365 Calories | 38.3g Carbohydrates |18.5g Fat | 20.2g Protein

INGREDIENTS:

1 Brioche

1 slice (2 ounces) Prosciutto

2 ounces artichoke hearts, in oil

Cream Cheese Spread Chive and Onion

1 large egg

Fresh chives

DIRECTIONS:

Preheat breakfast sandwich maker.

Cut Brioche in half. Place one-half, split side up, into bottom ring of breakfast sandwich maker. Add Canadian bacon and artichokes.

In a small bowl, whisk egg.

Lower cooking plate and top ring. Add egg.

Spread cream cheese on remaining brioche half. Top with fresh chives. Place brioche, spread side down on top of egg.

Close cover. Cook 4 – 5 minutes. Gently rotate cooking plate handle away clockwise. Lift rings. Remove breakfast sandwich with a nylon spatula.

Monte Cristo Twist

"Great for breakfast, lunch, dinner or late night munchies. . .

Servings: 1

Prep Time: 5 Minutes

Cook Time: 5 Minutes

Per Serving: 403 Calories | 40.5g Carbohydrates |17.4g Fat | 20.9g Protein

INGREDIENTS:

2 slices frozen French toast

1 slices (1 ounce each) Swiss cheese

1 slice ham

Maple syrup (optional)

Powdered sugar (optional)

DIRECTIONS:

Preheat breakfast sandwich maker. .

Place one slice French toast in bottom ring of breakfast sandwich maker. Top with 1 slice Swiss cheese, 1 slice ham, and 1 slice Brick cheese. .

Lower cooking plate and top ring. Top with remaining slice of French toast. .

Close cover. Cook 4 – 5 minutes. Gently rotate cooking plate handle away clockwise. Lift rings. Remove breakfast sandwich with a plastic or nylon spatula.

Sprinkle with powdered sugar. Serve with maple syrup.

Chorizo Egg Torta

"Creamy gooey goodness from the Avocado and cheeses add incredible highlights to the spicy chorizo.

Servings: 1

Prep Time: 5 Minutes

Cook Time: 5 Minutes

Per Serving: 412 Calories | 21.7g Carbohydrates |29.9g Fat | 17.7g Protein

INGREDIENTS:

1 round flatbread, sliced crosswise

1 Chorizo Sausage patty, cooked

1/2 Avocado, cleaned, pitted and sliced

2 ounces Monterey Jack, shredded

1 Tbsp Feta cheese or Queso Fresco, crumbled

1 large egg

DIRECTIONS:

Preheat breakfast sandwich maker.

Place the bottom slice of flatbread, split side up, into bottom ring of breakfast sandwich maker. Add Chorizo sausage patty. Add Avocado slices, Monterey Jack and Feta to top of sausage.

In small bowl, gently whisk egg.

Lower cooking plate and top ring.

Add whisked egg to cooking plate. Top with remaining flatbread slice, split side down.

Close cover. Cook 4 – 5 minutes. Gently rotate cooking plate handle away clockwise. Lift rings. Remove breakfast sandwich with a plastic or nylon spatula.

Provençal with Bacon and Gruyere

"Aioli adds just the right garlicky twist to the bacon, gruyere and hearty bread. I prefer to use Sourdough, instead of French, because of the added digestive and nutritional quality of Sourdough. Many gluten-intolerant people are able to eat Sourdough bread too.

Servings: 1

Prep Time: 10 Minutes

Cook Time: 5 Minutes

Per Serving: 570 Calories | 34.7g Carbohydrates | 33.8g Fat | 29.8g Protein

INGREDIENTS:

2 slices, French or Sourdough Bread

2 slices thick cut Bacon, cooked

1 slice (1 ounce) Gruyere

1 large egg

1 Tbsp Aioli

1/2 cup Arugula

DIRECTIONS:

Preheat breakfast sandwich maker.

Place one-slice Sourdough or French bread into bottom ring of breakfast sandwich maker. Add 2 slices each of thick cut bacon and the Gruyere cheese.

Lower cooking plate and top ring.

Crack egg into top ring and piece egg yolk. Top with Arugula.

Spread Aioli on remaining bread slice. Add bread to top of egg and Arugula, spread side down.

Close cover. Cook 4 – 5 minutes. Gently rotate cooking plate handle away clockwise. Lift rings. Remove breakfast sandwich with a plastic or nylon spatula.

Southwestern Chicken Sandwich

"Start the day with a healthy taste of the southwest.

Servings: 1

Prep Time: 10 Minutes

Cook Time: 5 Minutes

Per Serving: 583 Calories | 23.2g Carbohydrates | 42.1g Fat | 23.6g Protein

INGREDIENTS:

1 croissant, sliced

1 Applegate Farms natural chicken patty, cooked

1 slice Monterey Jack cheese

1 tbsp Chipotle mayo

1 large egg

Arugula (optional)

Tomato slice (optional)

Red onion slice (optional)

DIRECTIONS:

Preheat breakfast sandwich maker.

Place bottom half of croissant, split side up, into bottom ring of breakfast sandwich maker. Add cooked chicken patty – we used Applegate Farms patties, but any good crispy natural chicken patty will work. Top with Monterey Jack.

In small bowl, gently whisk egg.

Lower cooking plate and top ring.

Add whisked egg to cooking plate. Top with tomato slice, Arugula and red onion slice if desired.

Spread Chipotle mayo on top slice of croissant. Place croissant, spread side down on top of egg.

Close cover. Cook 4 – 5 minutes. Gently rotate cooking plate handle away clockwise. Lift rings. Remove breakfast sandwich with a nylon spatula.

Anytime Quesadillas

"For breakfast, lunch, dinner or that late night snack, these quesadillas are the perfect treat for anyone.

Servings: 1

Prep Time: 10 Minutes

Cook Time: 5 Minutes

Per Serving: 399 Calories | 23.8g Carbohydrates |23.7g Fat | 23.3g Protein

INGREDIENTS:

2 mini Tortillas

1 slice Bacon, cooked and crumbled

1 ounce white Cheddar cheese, shredded

1 tbsp onions, chopped

1 tbsp green pepper, chopped

1/4 Tbsp butter, (or lite cooking spray if desired)

Ground cumin, pinch

Salt to taste

1 large egg

Sour cream (optional)

Salsa (optional)

DIRECTIONS:

Preheat breakfast sandwich maker.

Place one-tortilla into bottom ring of breakfast sandwich maker

In small frying pan, melt butter and sauté onions and peppers until soft and translucent; about 3 minutes.

In small bowl, whisk eggs with fork. Add sautéed onions and peppers to eggs. Stir in pinch of cumin and salt.

Lower cooking plate and top ring. Add egg mixture.

Top with remaining tortilla.

Close cover. Cook 4 – 5 minutes. Gently rotate cooking plate handle away clockwise. Lift rings. Remove breakfast sandwich with a plastic, nylon or wooden spatula.

Optionally top with sour cream and salsa.

Green Eggs and Ham

"Well not exactly green eggs, but a little bit of whimsy is a great way to start the day. Plus you get some of your daily power greens in early.

Servings: 1

Prep Time: 7 Minutes

Cook Time: 5 Minutes

Per Serving: 338 Calories | 27.3g Carbohydrates |17.1g Fat | 19.2g Protein

INGREDIENTS:

1 English muffin

1/2 cup baby spinach, washed and chopped

1 tsp olive oil

1 slice Cheddar cheese

1 slice ham

1 egg

Fresh basil (optional)

DIRECTIONS:

Preheat breakfast sandwich maker.

Place one-half muffin, split side up, into bottom ring of breakfast sandwich maker. Add 1 slice each of Ham and Cheddar cheese.

In small sauté pan heat olive oil. Add spinach and sauté until just softened. Remove from heat.

In small bowl, blend spinach and egg together with a fork.

Lower cooking plate and top ring. Add egg and spinach mixture.

Top with remaining muffin half, split side down.

Close cover. Cook 4 – 5 minutes. Gently rotate cooking plate handle away clockwise. Lift rings. Remove breakfast sandwich with a plastic or nylon spatula.

Cranberry Bagel Sausage Treat

"The mix of cranberry and sausage gives this sandwich a tasty sweet and spicy twist. You can also add some cranberry chutney as a topping to give this one added zest.

Servings: 1

Prep Time: 5 Minutes

Cook Time: 5 Minutes

Per Serving: 676 Calories | 78.7g Carbohydrates | 30.5g Fat | 24.1g Protein

INGREDIENTS:

1 sausage patty, fully cooked

1 large egg

1 small cranberry bagel, split

1 tablespoons cream cheese

1 teaspoon chopped green onions or chives

Cranberry chutney (optional)

DIRECTIONS:

Preheat breakfast sandwich maker.

Spread cut side of bagel halves with cream cheese

Place one-half bagel, spread side up, into bottom ring of breakfast sandwich maker. Add cooked sausage patty.

Lower cooking plate and top ring. Add egg. Pierce top of egg with a toothpick or pointed plastic utensil.

Sprinkle egg with chopped chives or green onion. Top with remaining bagel half, spread side down.

Close cover. Cook 4 – 5 minutes. Gently rotate cooking plate handle away clockwise. Lift rings. Remove breakfast sandwich with a nylon spatula.

Optional: dip sandwich in cranberry chutney.

Muffuletta Egg Sandwich

"A twist on a New Orleans favorite.

Servings: 1

Prep Time: 10 Minutes

Cook Time: 5 Minutes

Per Serving: 473 Calories | 41.8g Carbohydrates |22.8g Fat | 24.9g Protein

INGREDIENTS:

1 slice ham, cooked

1 egg

2 slices French bread

1 slice provolone cheese

1 tbsp pimento-stuffed green olives, chopped

1 tbsp roasted red bell pepper, drained and chopped

DIRECTIONS:

Preheat breakfast sandwich maker.

Place one slice of French bread into bottom ring of breakfast sandwich maker. Add ham slice. Sprinkle pimentos and peppers over ham. Top with provolone cheese slice.

Lower cooking plate and top ring. Add egg. Pierce top of egg with a toothpick or pointed plastic utensil.

Top with remaining French bread slice.

Close cover. Cook 4 – 5 minutes. Gently rotate cooking plate handle away clockwise. Lift rings. Remove breakfast sandwich with nylon spatula.

California BLT

"Yummy Bacon, Lettuce and Tomato made with a morning twist.

Servings: 1

Prep Time: 5 Minutes

Cook Time: 5 Minutes

Per Serving: 357 Calories | 37.1g Carbohydrates | 13.4g Fat | 20.0g Protein

INGREDIENTS:

3 slices bacon, cooked and cut to fit

1 egg

1 pita bread, cut in half

1 slice tomato

2 leaves romaine lettuce

2 tbsp yogurt

DIRECTIONS:

Preheat breakfast sandwich maker.

Cut pita bread in half. Spread each cut side with yogurt. Place one-half pita, split side up, into bottom ring of breakfast sandwich maker. Add bacon, tomato and lettuce leaves.

In small bowl, lightly whisk egg. Lower cooking plate and top ring. Add egg to cooking ring.

Top with remaining pita top, split side down.

Close cover. Cook 4 – 5 minutes. Gently rotate cooking plate handle away clockwise. Lift rings. Remove breakfast sandwich with a nylon or plastic spatula.

Turkey Sausage, Pepper Jack Cheese and Veggies on Flatbread

"Turkey, veggies and cheese with a kick. . .oh my. . .

Servings: 1

Prep Time: 10 Minutes

Cook Time: 5 Minutes

Per Serving: 408 Calories | 39.0g Carbohydrates |17.2g Fat | 37.9g Protein

INGREDIENTS:

2 flatbread rounds

1 turkey sausage patty, cooked

1 slice pepper jack cheese

1 small tomato, diced

1 tbsp fresh basil, chopped

1 egg

DIRECTIONS:

Preheat breakfast sandwich maker.

Place flatbread round into bottom ring of breakfast sandwich maker. Add turkey sausage patty and pepper jack cheese.

In a small bowl blend together egg, tomato and basil. Lower cooking plate and top ring. Add egg mixture to cooking plate.

Top with remaining flatbread round.

Close cover. Cook 4 – 5 minutes. Gently rotate cooking plate handle away clockwise. Lift rings. Remove breakfast sandwich with a nylon spatula.

Turkey Cobb Sandwich

"A take on the traditional cobb salad with gooey goodness.

Servings: 1

Prep Time: 5 Minutes

Cook Time: 5 Minutes

Per Serving: 542 Calories | 30.6g Carbohydrates | 29.7g Fat | 37.0g Protein

INGREDIENTS:

1 sandwich bun, medium

3 oz deli turkey breast slices

2 slices bacon, cooked

1/4 avocado, sliced

2 oz blue cheese

1 egg

DIRECTIONS:

Preheat breakfast sandwich maker.

Place lower half of bun into bottom ring of breakfast sandwich maker. Add turkey breast, bacon (large crumbles), avocado and blue cheese.

Lower cooking plate and top ring. Add egg. Pierce top of egg with a toothpick or pointed plastic utensil. Top with top of bun.

Close cover. Cook 4 – 5 minutes. Gently rotate cooking plate handle away clockwise. Lift rings. Remove sandwich with a spatula.

Kick'n Hot Late Night Sandwich

"Harissa paste adds the kick to this sandwich. Harissa is a red pepper-based paste used in North African cuisine.

Servings: 1

Prep Time: 5 Minutes

Cook Time: 5 Minutes

Per Serving: 379 Calories | 34.7g Carbohydrates |19.4g Fat | 31.8g Protein

INGREDIENTS:

2 flatbread slices

2 slices Applewood smoked bacon, cooked

Harissa paste, to taste

1 slice cucumber, cut crosswise (optional)

1 egg

DIRECTIONS:

Preheat breakfast sandwich maker.

Spread Harissa on flatbread. Place one slice flatbread, spread side up, into bottom ring of breakfast sandwich maker. Add cucumber and bacon.

Lower cooking plate and top ring. Add egg. Pierce top of egg with a toothpick or pointed plastic utensil.

Top with remaining flatbread.

Close cover. Cook 4 – 5 minutes. Gently rotate cooking plate handle away clockwise. Lift rings. Remove breakfast sandwich with a plastic, nylon or wooden spatula.

Smoked Salmon, Cream Cheese and Capers with Egg and Bagel

"Almost like your favorite delicatessen with your morning egg.

Servings: 1

Prep Time: 5 Minutes

Cook Time: 5 Minutes

Per Serving: 387 Calories | 37.3g Carbohydrates | 15.0g Fat | 24.9g Protein

INGREDIENTS:

1 small bagel, cut in half

2 ounces smoked salmon

2 tbsp cream cheese with chive and onion

1/2 tsp capers

1 egg

DIRECTIONS:

Preheat breakfast sandwich maker.

Spread cream cheese on bagel halves. Place one-half bagel, cream cheese side up, into bottom ring of breakfast sandwich maker. Add smoked salmon.

In a small bowl, lightly beat egg; add capers to egg. Lower cooking plate and top ring. Add beaten egg mixture.

Top with remaining bagel half, spread side down.

Close cover. Cook 4 – 5 minutes. Gently rotate cooking plate handle away clockwise. Lift rings. Remove breakfast sandwich with a plastic, nylon or wooden spatula.

Prosciutto Asparagus Eggs Benedict

"Delectable, creamy take on a classic egg dish. . ..

Servings: 1

Prep Time: 10 Minutes

Cook Time: 5 Minutes

Per Serving: 508 Calories | 39.0g Carbohydrates |20.7g Fat | 40.7g Protein

INGREDIENTS:

1/2 English muffin

3 slices prosciutto, thinly sliced

3 asparagus stalks, broiled

1 tsp olive oil

2 tbsp Greek yogurt, unflavored

1 tsp half and half or milk

1 tsp Dijon mustard

1/8 tsp lemon juice

Sea salt

Chives, snipped

1 egg

DIRECTIONS:

Preheat oven to 450 degrees. Line baking sheet with aluminum foil. Lay asparagus on baking sheet; coat with olive oil. Sprinkle with sea salt.

Place in oven for 5-7 minutes. Remove from oven and cut into 3-inch pieces.

Preheat breakfast sandwich maker.

In small cup, combine yogurt, mustard and lemon juice. Set aside.

Place muffin half into bottom ring of breakfast sandwich maker. Layer with asparagus.

Lower cooking plate and top ring. Add egg. Pierce top of egg with a toothpick or pointed plastic utensil.

Top with chives.

Close cover. Cook 4 – 5 minutes. Gently rotate cooking plate handle away clockwise. Lift rings. Remove breakfast sandwich with a nylon spatula.

Drizzle yogurt mixture over top egg.

Maple Bread Pudding Sandwich

"The latest trendy breakfast sandwich uses slices of bread pudding for the ultimate in decadence. . .umm and calories. . . You can get very creative by using a variety of dense stale breads for your pudding.

Servings: 1

Prep Time: 10 Minutes

Cook Time: 5 Minutes

Per Serving: 993 Calories | 94.3g Carbohydrates |39.2g Fat | 56.4g Protein

INGREDIENTS:

2 slices Bread Pudding (recipe follows)

1 pork sausage patty

1 thick slice chipotle cheddar cheese

1 egg

DIRECTIONS:

Preheat breakfast sandwich maker.

Place one-bread pudding into bottom ring of breakfast sandwich maker. Layer pork sausage patty and chipotle cheddar cheese.

Lower cooking plate and top ring. Add egg. Pierce top of egg with a toothpick or pointed plastic utensil.

Top with remaining bread pudding.

Close cover. Cook 4 – 5 minutes. Gently rotate cooking plate handle away clockwise. Lift rings. Remove breakfast sandwich with a plastic, nylon or wooden spatula.

5-Minute Bread Pudding

"Moist goodness anytime anywhere and oh so fast and easy to make.

Servings: 2

Prep Time: 5 Minutes

Cook Time: 5 Minutes

Per Serving: 359 Calories | 39.9g Carbohydrates |17.8g Fat | 11.4g Protein

INGREDIENTS:

4 slices dense stale bread

2 eggs

4 tbsp Maple syrup

4 tbsp yogurt

2 tbsp butter, melted

Pinch of Cinnamon

DIRECTIONS:

Tear bread in to small chunks; divide recipe in half and place in two ramekins.

In a small bowl blend butter (melted), egg, syrup, yogurt and cinnamon. Pour mixture over bread chunks and move bread bits to make sure mixture fills in openings around bread. Do not stir.

Microwave on high for 2 minutes or until firm. Let cool a few minutes to absorb flavors.

Glazed Donut Sandwich

"A donut by any other name can still be a donut sandwich of course...

Servings: 1

Prep Time: 5 Minutes

Cook Time: 5 Minutes

Per Serving: 466 Calories | 25.6g Carbohydrates | 31.3g Fat | 20.6g Protein

INGREDIENTS:

1 glazed donut, cut in half

3 slices bacon, cooked

1 slice sharp cheddar

1 egg

DIRECTIONS:

Preheat breakfast sandwich maker.

Place one-half donut, split side up, into bottom ring of breakfast sandwich maker. Cook and cut bacon slices in half. Add bacon slices and the slice of sharp cheddar cheese to top of donut.

Lower cooking plate and top ring. Add egg. Pierce top of egg with a toothpick or pointed plastic utensil.

Top with remaining donut half, split side down.

Close cover. Cook 4 – 5 minutes. Gently rotate cooking plate handle away clockwise. Lift rings. Remove breakfast sandwich with a plastic, nylon or wooden spatula.

ABOUT THE AUTHOR

Jennifer Williams spent years working in large multinational corporations traveling around the World. She was able to explore many different cultures and lifestyles during these travels. During one of her last excursions, she realized she knew more about the countries she visited and worked in than the city in which she called home. It was time to take another turn.

She left the corporate life to spend time with family and friends and pursue her many interests. Now, she has spent the last decade cultivating these passions, many relating to home, food and health. She writes about many of these topics and is a syndicated contributor with the eMJayMedia network.

Jennifer is an exhaustive researcher and has hands-on experience with the topics she covers. Her books are designed to help people find inspiration and answers to questions they have in everyday life.

Made in the USA
Lexington, KY
03 December 2013